50

PLUS

50

AND

ONE

QUOTES

1st Edition

Khalid Ibn Anderson

A Tribute To
Cognitive Engineering

Come Look Within

My Mind's Eye,

And See

The Wisdom

That Was Sent

To Elevate

Humanity.

A BOOK OF QUOTES

50

PLUS

50

AND ONE

QUOTES

1st Edition

50 PLUS 50 AND ONE QUOTES

KHALID IBN ANDERSON

A Tribute To Cognitive Engineering

LAZY GAL SWOFIYAH SELF PUBLISHING & THINGS LLC

This book is a collection of quotes written over the years. A collection of thoughts from the recess of my mind that I allow to fly regardless of my stationery position.

Copyright © 2025 by KHALIB IBN ANDERSON
50 PLUS 50 AND ONE QUOTES: A Tribute To Cognitive Engineering

Cover art by Khalid Ibn Anderson
Cover design by Tanya Chambers of IGSS-P&T LLC
Editing: Lazy Gal Swofiyah Self-Publishing & Things LLC

This book is the paperback edition of 50 PLUS 50 AND ONE QUOTES: A Tribute to Cognitive Engineering, published by LAZY GAL SWOFIYAH SELF-PUBLISHING THINGS LLC

Rochester, NY 14609

Published and printed in the United States Of America

LAZY GAL SWOFIYAH SELF-PUBLISHING & THINGS LLC
https://www.lazygalswofiyahself-publishingthingsllc.com

Library of Congress Control Number: 2025913337

ISBN: 979-8-9989798-2-8

Dedication

My wife, my fire, so much could be said, so much should be said. The best of all I could ever say is, "May all your Dreams and Desires be fulfilled in this life and the next. Ameen."

To all those who were out there for me, I thank you.

To those who gave me the nourishment needed to stand up and survive every and all elements: Kevin Louis Anderson, Julia Mae Davis, Juliette Elizabeth Anderson, Nora Lucille Davis, Barbara J. Mc Cullough, Richard Sylvester Anderson, Jacqueline Knowlin, Patricia Knowlin, Denise Knowlin, Ervin Smalls, Sr., Gerald Fabien Anderson, Sr., Mark Anthony Anderson, Frances Ann Smalls, Delaine Cook-Green.

With gratitude I say thank you.

YOU ARE NOT MISSING ANYTHING

Introduction

Words, phrases, and profound quotes
have existed since the dawn of
humanity. To engage in a debate over
their lasting significance would not be
nearly as crucial as discussing their
foundational cultivating principles. As
you delve deeper into this text, you will
undoubtedly notice how I have woven
my unique perceptions into the
narrative. However, I genuinely do not
wish to distort your understanding or
diminish the challenge inherent in your
exploration of these comprehensive
notions.

I would highly recommend that you
share these moral precepts with a
relative, friend, or romantic partner, as
dialogue can often enhance
comprehension. Just keep in mind that
there is not a singular answer that holds
true in isolation. Embrace and relish the
gift of thoughtful reflection. Understand
that when you broaden your mind, you
indeed expand your horizons and
limitless possibilities. These insights

and quotes were carefully crafted over an extensive eighteen-year journey of confronting life head-on and achieving triumph.

WHO
CRIES?

1. Remember, routes of illusions and dead ends; never travel that course again.

2. In prosperity our friends know us, and in adversity we know our friends.

3. Power is being able to identify the answer, not to over analyze.

4. Over analyzing leads to confusion and blaming, be ready to adapt and change as situation change.

5. No gift is to be taken for granted, is not life the ultimate gift?

6. Familiarity can make one comfortable, which can bring about one's downfall due to a false sense of security.

7. Confidence unchecked becomes arrogance hated by the rest.

8. Maintaining a proper sense of reality will equip you with the proper instincts to inevitably move forward.

9. Loud mouths never accomplish anything except making noise.

10. Never allow your ego
to make you so big that
you have to look down
upon other's.

11. Always have a back up plan, followed by a back up plan, followed by a back up plan.

12. Nothing last forever, so do your best with what you have while you have it.

13. Keep your goals active, do not fear the unknown.

14. Identify your strength, and acknowledge the trials you have already won in any arena.

15. Failure is not to be
feared, as it is not an
option.

16. Courage is not to fear not, it is to be able to act in the face of fear.

17. To change is to travel
into the unknown, the
unknown can be a depth of
darkness that breeds fear
or a time to trust upon The
All See'er.

18. Fear immobilizes and kills one's motivation.

19. Beware of being drawn back to familiar territory that holds no substance.

20. The frame work of our future is our children.

21. Keep your thoughts, attitudes and actions positive and you will be prosperous.

22. When you change
what you believe, you
change what you can do.

23. Letting go of you past,
will allow you to grab
your future.

24. Keep the past in the rear view, it is only for reflection not to give correction.

25. Human beliefs and emotions can cloud one's judgements, making life complicated.

26. Learn to read the handwriting on the wall, and life will not be such a mystery.

27. You can take the clock off the wall, throw away the batteries, do as you may; you can never stop time.

28. Once you expand your mind, you expand your possibilities.

29. Consequences are the fruit produced from the seeds of your actions. Whether they are ripe or rotten is up to you.

30. If change is needed in any aspect, know that change must start with you first.

31. If there were no problems, what need would there be for wisdom or courage.

32. He who understands how to deal with circumstances, will not allow things to do him harm.

33. Always remember the moment you feel like giving up, could very well be the moment you didn't need to.

34. Wrong turns in life never lead to the right direction.

35. Never close the doors on hope.

36. Before you can enjoy
the fruits of your future,
you must labor in your
present.

37. The pain of our consciousness can become so severe that it can lead one into a state of unconsciousness.

38. Do not think about
what you can lose, think
about what you can gain.

39. Life is not about perfection, it's about the journey of striving to be morally perfect.

40. Obstacles are only opportunities to be creative.

41. Change your thinking
and you change your life.

42. Life is full of trials
and with every trial comes
two possible results, either
you pass or fail.

43. Our leadership potential is challenged with changes.

44. The struggle of life started with the first stroke and will not end until you croak.

45. Everyday is a lifetime,
how many have you
wasted?

46. The arrow will not hit the target, unless it leaves the bow.

47. Water is not purified
unless it's in constant
motion; know that you are
water.

48. A man who feels the need to explain himself, is unsure of himself.

49. There is good in everyday, focus on that good and it will get you through the toughness of the day.

50. No one knows what
the future holds, so extend
your energy to holding
onto today.

51. A jewel is worthless
unless someone embraces
and wears it.

52. Tough times do not last forever, tough people do.

53. Establish committees,
never close a deal without
seeking advice.

54. Sincerity is a
motivational energy that
has no boundaries.

55. Knowledge is not new, only today is and what you decide to do with it.

56. Hatred is a fire that burns everybody, while love is the vaccine that soothes everybody.

57. A frown is like an offensive odor, while a smile brings the fragrance of your perfect odor.

58. A friend can be a foe,
or a foe can be a friend, so
greet everyone the same:
No smiles or frowns, wear
a smooth grin to the end.

59. He who is in control
has control. Control
yourself and you control
your surroundings.

60. Before you ask a
question, relax and allow
your environment to give
you the answer.

61. Take the time to see things for what they are, and not what they appear to be.

62. Emotions can blind your view, while intellect can give you the ability to see things through.

63. Something we all want, yet we should never look for it: "LOVE". It is always near, yet it will only appear when there's no fear.

64. Fiction and non fiction have so much in common, that only three letters distinguish them: "NON" or the "ONE" telling the story.

65. It takes time and effort
to get it right, while it only
takes a matter of seconds
to think you got it right.

66. Maintain the soul of your youth, while you develop the soul of an elder, learn how to balance the two.

67. Stay positive, productive, and you will be prosperous.

68. There is so much power in being humble, that's why it takes so much power to be so.

69. Looking to make a
relationship work? Give
more than you take and
communicate,
communicate.

70. Isolation can be a
prize, or it can bring about
one's demise.

71. Life is a paradox, more mysterious than pandora's box.

72. Instead of seeking to destroy the snake that you see, let it be, soon it will flee.

73. Every seed planted in life has the potential to grow, be it physical, mental or spiritual.

74. Know that every seed
is an action, word or
thought, that can grow to
be destructive or
beneficial.

75. Knowledge of life can come from a far or near, one who is less desired, or one who is very dear.

76. Is it not true that a
stranger is only a friend
that one has yet to meet.

77. A spider's web is beautiful, yet dangerous. A spider's web is   fragile, yet strong. A spider's web is a place for comfort and security. So is love, all of the above.

78. Stop trying to correct
life, and its affairs. Spend
more time correcting
yourself and your affairs.

79. Curiosity can be the gateway to no return, while hope can be the bridge that leads you home.

80. Be your own
inspiration and you will
have no limitations.

81. Sacrifices will be made, and prices will be paid in order to enjoy the ultimate parade.

82. Do you want to be great? Then simply except every challenge.

83. The battles within life may be great, just remember the reward for overcoming will always be greater.

84. Wherever you find
rights, you will find
responsibilities.

85. You will drown in
your problems if you
attempt to swallow them.

86. There's nothing
wrong with progressing, as
long as one's priorities line
up.

87. Stop running around,
let the dust settle down,
and you will see your way
clearly.

88. Spend more time
perfecting your character,
instead of perfecting your
appearance.

89. Everything is not always what it appears to be, but it is always the way it should be.

90. Family has little to do
with blood and genes, the
answer is in character.
Know the role and the part
can be yours.

91. The demons of your
past will always haunt
you, unless you hunt them.

92. The reason of rational is more concrete when collaborated.

93. Tragedy can be a
piercing knife that
destroys your life, or a tool
that enables you to
overcome all strife.

94. One brief moment of
contact can establish a
lifetime connection.

95. A sharp tongue
Untamed can be the blade
that cuts its own throat.

96. A kiss can lead to the doorway of bliss, or to the ultimate dismiss.

97. Perception is not the ability to see, it's the ability to see what you perceive.

98. The decisions of right or wrong, should always be determined by benefit or conflict.

99. Life is measured by
the ruler of productivity.

WHO CRIES?

100. Life is definitely not a game, yet it can be one heck of a show, giving you the opportunity to choose your role. Make sure it is a nominee pick.

101. When we get to the end of ourselves, is when ALLAH begins.

Reflections

As you have made it to the end of my thoughtful visions, know that you have now made it the beginning of your own.

Take these thoughtful seeds and take care to plant them wisely, and let discipline and patience be your tools of cultivation.

I wish I could be with every reader to witness the miraculous power to thought in action.

Perhaps our paths will cross, and our actions will speak for themselves. Giving is the ultimate connection of consciousness.

With love and gratitude, I thank life. For it was life itself that taught, inspired and edged me forward to complete this endeavor, making it possible to be in your hands today

With Love

Sincerely,

Khalid I. Anderson

About the Author

Khalid Ibn Anderson was born and
raised in the City of Rochester, New
York. He attended Frederick Douglass
School, followed by Benjamin Franklin
High School. The invaluable years spent
in these educational institutions shaped
his character, teaching him to be a
strong, unapologetic male.

At the age of nineteen, he found
himself in the New York State
Correctional Facilities (NYSCF), where
he remained until reaching the age of
thirty-six. During this transformative
period, he learned that life was truly
what he made of it, gaining profound
insights about his existence. It was in
this reflective space that Khalid Ibn

Anderson delved deep within himself to uncover the true meaning of life. He harnessed the knowledge gained from his extensive meditation practice and evolved into the accomplished writer he is today.

When he's not passionately immersed in writing, he enjoys indulging in the great outdoors, engaging in activities that ignite his spirit, such as fishing, hunting, cooking, or having meaningful conversations with others.

KHALID IBN ANDERSON
mr.khalidanderson@yahoo.com